1 Baker Street Underground Station
  ("Planetarium & Madame Tussaud…
2 Statue of Sherlock Holmes
3 The Bar Linda Cafe
4 Sherlock Holmes Museum
5 The London Beatles Store
6 Westminster Library
7 Bickenhall Street
8 N° 109 Baker Street
9 Sherlock Holmes Hotel

15 N° 2 Upper Wimpole Street
   (Conan Doyle's Practice)
16 N° 15 Welbeck Street
17 Harley Street
18 N° 9 Queen Anne Street
19 Langham Hotel
20 Oxford Circus Underground Station

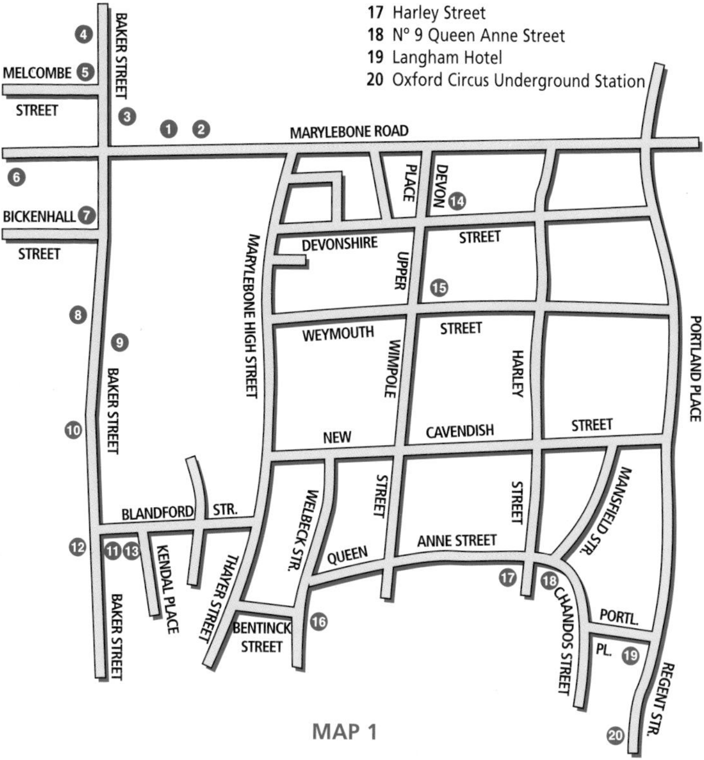

C000066424

MARYLEBONE ROAD

BAKER STREET

MELCOMBE

STREET

BICKENHALL

STREET

MARYLEBONE HIGH STREET

DEVONSHIRE

DEVON

PLACE

STREET

UPPER

WEYMOUTH STREET

WIMPOLE

STREET

HARLEY

NEW CAVENDISH STREET

STREET

PORTLAND PLACE

BAKER STREET

BLANDFORD STR.

KENDAL PLACE

THAYER STREET

WELBECK STR.

QUEEN ANNE STREET

MANSFIELD STR.

BENTINCK STREET

CHANDOS STREET

PORTL.

PL.

REGENT STR.

BAKER STREET

MAP 1

STAGE 1: BAKER STREET TO OXFORD CIRCUS

Directions: Start this Walk at Baker Street Underground Station, which can be reached via the Bakerloo, Jubilee, Metropolitan, Hammersmith & City, and Circle Lines. Exit Baker Street Underground Station at the "Planetarium and Madame Tussauds" Exit on Marylebone Road ❶. This is where the Walk starts. (If you leave the Station from any other exit, please walk around the Station to Marylebone Road to this Exit.)

Baker Street Underground Station: To the left of the station entrance is a statue of Sherlock Holmes ❷, which was commissioned by the Sherlock Holmes Society in 1999. The monument, which depicts a standing Holmes at the Reichenback Falls, was sculpted by John Doubleday.

Directions: Walk back to the entrance of the Underground Station, and walk approximately 30 metres further to the corner of Baker Street, outside the HSBC Bank. Turn right into Baker Street and continue to N°224, which is the Bar Linda Cafe. ❸

Bar Linda Cafe:
This friendly Italian Cafe has been part of the Baker Street scene for many years and has many prints and pictures relating to Sherlock Holmes and Baker Street on its walls.

Directions: Cross Baker Street , on your right is the Sherlock Holmes Museum ❹

Sherlock Holmes Museum:
There is often a friendly guard, dressed as a Victorian London Bobby outside the Museum. This interesting Museum (upstairs) contains several Canonical rooms and an elaborate reconstruction of the famous sitting room, which Holmes and Watson occupied at N° 221B Baker Street. On the ground floor is a comprehensive gift shop, stocking a wide range of items related to our heroes and their many adventures. The museum also displays a unique waxworks exhibition of characters from the Sherlock Holmes stories.

The famous study overlooking Baker Street has been portrayed in so many films and is located on the first floor above a flight of 17 steps. Visitors can sit in Mr Holmes's armchair by the fireside and pose for photographs. His private bedroom, which adjoins the study, displays many of his most precious possessions including his deerstalker, magnifying glass, violin, Persian slippers and his disguises.

Directions: Exit the Sherlock Holmes Museum. Turn right and stop at N°231 Baker Street, which is the London Beatles Store. ❺

The London Beatles Store: The first and only Beatles shop in London. Well worth a visit if you are a Beatles fan. John Lennon's 1965 book of nonsensical stories, entitled "A Spaniard in the Works" contained a parody of Arthur Conan Doyle's writing style ("The Singularge Experience of Miss Anne Duffield").

Directions: Cross Melcombe Street and continue along Baker Street until you arrive at the traffic lights. Cross Marylebone Road. [If you turn right down Marylebone Road, on the left is the Westminster Library ❻ *. Unfortunately, you cannot visit the Sherlock Holmes Collection at Westminster Library, unless you first make an appointment. (See "USEFUL INFORMATION" section)].*
Continue directly ahead into this older section of Baker Street keeping on the right hand side and stop at the corner of Baker Street and Bickenhall Street ❼

Baker Street:
"I have my eye on a suite in Baker Street"
This southern (older) section of Baker Street, which we are about to explore, was built in 1755 and was the Baker Street that Holmes and Watson would have known.

The north side of Baker Street containing the London Beatles Store etc. was, in Holmes' time, called Upper Baker Street and was renamed Baker Street on 1 January 1930. Most authorities acknowledge that Upper Baker Street never had an address even close to N° 221 Baker Street at the time of Holmes and Watson.

However, to confuse this issue further, there is a preserved piece of the original manuscript from "A Study in Scarlet", in which the address for N° 221B is specified as being in Upper Baker Street. This is, however the only time that this famous address had been linked to Upper Baker Street.

Directions: Cross Bickenhall Street and stop a few metres further along outside N° 109 Baker Street ❽ *(next to Post Office) which is one of the more authentic and attractive looking, if not the most plausible, contenders for N° 221B Baker Street.*

N° 109 Baker Street:

> *"Five minutes had not passed before we were flying*
> *in a Hansom down Baker Street."* (TDLFC)

This building has 3 upper storeys, a brick attic and possibly the only undeveloped ground floor in the whole of Baker Street (the others have been converted into shops and offices). The only original architectural piece missing from this house is the black iron railings that would have formed a front yard outside the property.

Directions: Cross Baker Street. Turn right and a little further along on the left hand side is the Sherlock Holmes Hotel ❾

Sherlock Holmes Hotel:
A good place for a break. The Hotel welcomes non-resident guests and there are many Sherlockian prints and paintings of interest to see. There are also two places to take some refreshment: the Sherlock's bar (where snacks and drinks can be ordered) and the Sherlock's Grill (which is more formal and offers full dinners).

Directions: Exit the Hotel. Turn left, continue and cross Paddington Street, stopping at N° 82 Baker Street. If you look to the other side of Baker Street at N° 79, you will see a well known Kosher restaurant called Rubens ❿

Rubens: This building was once the original Baker Street pharmacy. It is commonly thought that this was the local pharmacy, which Conan Doyle regularly visited.

Directions: Continue along Baker Street and cross Dorset Street, continue. cross Blandford Street and stop at N° 32 Baker Street, which is on the left. This is the front view of the most popular contender for Camden House ⓫*, which was the Empty House that Holmes and Watson entered into in "The Empty House".*

N° 32 Baker Street (Site of Camden House or The Empty House – front view):
The building would have, in Holmes' time, been a complete house, and looked similar to N° 109 Baker Street ❽. It would have also had black railings outside. Holmes and Watson entered the Empty House from the rear ⓭ which you will visit shortly.

Directions: Opposite Camden House on the opposite side of Baker Street, between N°s 19-35, is a block of offices of Marks and Spencer's ⓬*. It was here, at what was N° 21 Baker Street, that many believe was the site of N° 221B Baker Street where Holmes and Watson lived.*

Site of N° 221B Baker Street:
> *"We met next day as he had arranged, and inspected the rooms at N°221B, Baker Street ... and at once entered into possession."* (ASIS)

The location of Camden House **11** is crucial in determining the exact location of N° 221B Baker Street. Camden House has been located by following the directions and route taken by Holmes and Watson as told in "The Empty House". The route takes Holmes and Watson on a winding trail around Marylebone and eventually arrives at the back entrance of what is thought to be N° 32 Baker Street **13**, The Empty House (back entrance). There is also an important reference to N° 221B Baker Street in "The Empty House" (TEH), which indicates that Camden House and Holmes' lodgings were opposite each other:

> *"We are in Camden House, which stands opposite to our own old quarters".* (TEH)

Also in "The Empty House", you will recall that Colonel Sebastian Moran, the second most dangerous man in London, used an air-gun, from an upstairs open window at the front of Camden House **11** to shoot a soft-nosed bullet at Holmes in his lodgings **12**. The bullet hit the perfect wax model of Holmes, that Mrs Hudson had regularly turned so as to give the impression of a living person. If you look at the distance from the front of Camden House **11** to the site of N° 221B Baker Street **12**, you can imagine what a nice and easy shot Colonel Moran had.

More evidence comes from Dr Morris - a friend of Doyle's - who claimed that Doyle had asked him for suggestions on where his new character called Sherlock Holmes, in his new book ("A Study In Scarlet") could possibly live. Dr Morris suggested N° 21 Baker Street, where his own father had once lived. Doyle liked the idea of Baker Street and visited N° 21, which was then a private house. It is thought that Doyle decided to change the number to 221B Baker Street so as not to annoy the occupants of the house.

Directions: Return to Blandford Street. Turn right into Blandford Street and turn first right into a small cobblestoned street called Kendal Place. Enter and, on the right, at N° 14, is what is thought to be the rear entrance of Camden House **13** *and The Empty House that Holmes and Watson entered*

N° 14 Kendal Place (rear view of Camden House or The Empty House):
> *"Here he turned swiftly down a narrow passage, passed through a wooden gate into a deserted yard, and then opened with a key the back door of a house. We entered together and he closed it behind us."* (TEH)

Directions: Return to Blandford Street. Turn right and continue. Cross Manchester Street and continue along Blandford Street until the very end and you arrive at Marylebone High Street. Cross Marylebone High Street using the zebra crossing and turn left and continue on the right hand side for approximately 500 metres. Turn right into Devonshire Street. Cross the road and continue on the left. Turn into the third road on the left, which is Devonshire Place. On the right hand side is Nº 2 Devonshire Place **14**

Nº 2 Devonshire Place:
> *"There for £120 a year I got the use of a front room and part use of a waiting room. I was soon to find out that they were both waiting rooms, and now I know that it was better so."* (Sir Arthur Conan Doyle)

It was this building that Conan Doyle identified in his autobiography as being the location of his medical practice in 1891. The practice turned out to be unsuccessful and it was during the long gaps between patients that he wrote two his most memorable short stories "A Scandal in Bohemia" and "The Red Headed League".

However, nothing related to Conan Doyle is ever straightforward and there are many who believe that Conan Doyle made a mistake and wrongly identified the house in which he started to write. The alternative location is the next site.

Directions: Return to Devonshire Street. Cross the road and continue down Upper Wimpole Street on the left hand side. Stop at Nº 2 Upper Wimpole Street **15**, which is on the left.

Conan Doyle's Practice:
Up until only a few years ago this address would have meant nothing to Sherlockians. Today however, there are many that believe this is the actual address of Conan Doyle's practice. Notice the plaque which says he worked and wrote here in 1891.

Directions: Continue along Upper Wimpole Street a little further. Cross Weymouth Street and continue down Wimpole Street on the right until you come to New Cavendish Street. Turn right down New Cavendish Street, keeping on the right hand side and half way along cross the road at the zebra crossing. Turn right on the other side and turn first left into Welbeck Street. Continue down Welbeck Street on the right. Stop at the corner of Bentinck Street. Look across the road at the red brick house which is Nº 15 Welbeck Street **16**

Nº 15 Welbeck Street:

> *"My dear Watson, Professor Moriarty is not a man who lets the grass grow under his feet. I went out about midday to transact some business in Oxford Street. As I passed the corner which leads from Bentinck Street on to the Welbeck Street crossing, a two-horse van furiously driven whizzed round and was on me like a flash. I sprang for the footpath and saved myself by the fraction of a second. The van dashed round from Marylebone Lane and was gone in an instant."* (TFP)

It was here, just outside this beautiful house that an attempt was made on the life of Sherlock Holmes by Moriarty.

Directions: Return up Welbeck Street on the right hand side and turn first right into Queen Anne Street and continue on the left hand side, crossing Wimpole Street and stop at the junction with Harley Street **17**

Harley Street: It was at Nº 6 Harley Street (to your right) that Dr Moore Agar had his consulting rooms and from where he ordered Holmes to take a vacation if

> *"he wished to avert an absolute breakdown"*. (TDF)

Holmes decided to holiday in Cornwall, which led to his investigating the macabre deaths of the Tregennis family (TDF).

Directions: Cross Harley Street and continue along Queen Anne Street on the left hand side. Stop at the corner of Mansfield Street. Notice the house on the opposite side of the road at Nº 9 Queen Anne Street **18**

Nº 9 Queen Anne Street:

"I (Watson) was living in my rooms in Queen Anne Street at the time." (TIC)

Watson moved here after leaving Nº 221B Baker Street. The most favoured house for this location is Nº 9, with the black railings.

Directions: Cross Mansfield Street and continue into Chandos Street, keeping to the left. Turn first left into Portland Place, follow the road on the right hand side and on the corner is the famous Langham Hotel **19**

Langham Hotel:

Built in 1865, the Langham Hotel became the leading society hotel in London. Among its regular guests were Napoleon III of France (in exile), Mark Twain and Stanley Livingstone.

It was in the Hotel restaurant, in August 1889, that Conan Doyle had dinner with Dr Joseph Marshall Stoddart, an agent for the Philadelphia-based "Lippincott's Monthly Magazine". At this historic dinner, Doyle was first introduced to Oscar Wilde.

During the evening, both writers were commissioned to write new material. Doyle started work on "The Sign of Four" (TSOF) and Oscar Wilde was commissioned to write what turned out to be "The Picture Of Dorian Gray".

Arthur Conan Doyle agreed to write his story of 45,000 words for just £100 and it is believed he based the character called Thaddeus Sholto on the distinctive mannerisms and appearance of his new friend Oscar Wilde. Oscar Wilde apparently reciprocated and based one of his new characters called Alan Campbell (the young Scottish chemist who played the violin and lived with a housekeeper) on Conan Doyle.

It was at the Langham Hotel that Count Von Kramm (aka the King of Bohemia) in "A Study in Scarlet" (ASIS) and the Hon. Phillip Green in "The Disappearance of Lady Frances Carfax" (TDLFC) stayed. Another guest at the Hotel was Captain Arthur Morstan in "The Sign of Four" (TSOF):

> *"On reaching London I drove to the Langham and was informed that Captain Morstan was staying there, but had gone out for the night before and had not returned."* (TSOF)

Directions: Exit the Langham Hotel. Turn right into Regent Street, past All Souls Church, and keeping on the right hand side; continue until you reach Oxford Circus Underground Station **20**

Regent Street: Watson and Holmes followed Sir Henry Baskerville along Regent Street, as they in turn, were followed by a mysterious Hansom cab in "The Hound of the Baskerville's" (THOTB).

This is the end of Stage 1 of the Walk.

To continue with Stage 2 from Oxford Circus Underground Station, either:

Enter Oxford Circus Underground Station and get a train (Bakerloo Line), one stop only to Piccadilly Circus. On arrival follow the directions in Stage 2.
Or: *From Oxford Circus Underground Station, continue to walk directly ahead, crossing Oxford Street. Continue down the remainder of Regent Street, on the left hand side of the road (a 10 minute walk) to Piccadilly Circus and go to the statue of Eros to start Stage 2. (Note: You will walk past the Café Royal on Regent Street, which is site* **21** *in Stage 2).*

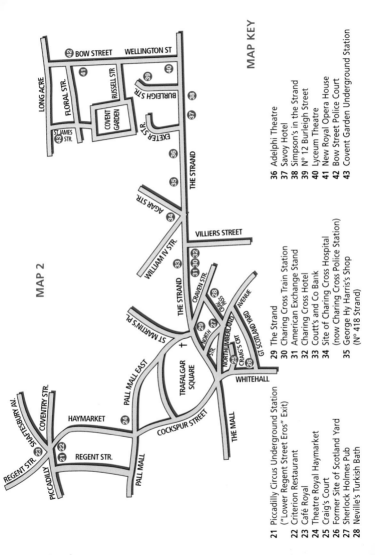

MAP 2

MAP KEY

21 Piccadilly Circus Underground Station ("Lower Regent Street Eros" Exit)
22 Criterion Restaurant
23 Café Royal
24 Theatre Royal Haymarket
25 Craig's Court
26 Former Site of Scotland Yard
27 Sherlock Holmes Pub
28 Neville's Turkish Bath

29 The Strand
30 Charing Cross Train Station
31 American Exchange Stand
32 Charing Cross Hotel
33 Coutt's and Co Bank
34 Site of Charing Cross Hospital (now Charing Cross Police Station)
35 George Hy Harris's Shop (N° 418 Strand)

36 Adelphi Theatre
37 Savoy Hotel
38 Simpson's in the Strand
39 N° 12 Burleigh Street
40 Lyceum Theatre
41 New Royal Opera House
42 Bow Street Police Court
43 Covent Garden Underground Station

Directions: Exit Piccadilly Circus Underground Station ㉑ *via the stairs labelled "Lower Regent Street Eros". Walk up the stairs to street level and turn left towards the statue of Eros. To the right of Eros is the Criterion Building, which houses the Criterion Theatre and further to the left is the famous Criterion Restaurant* ㉒

Criterion Restaurant:

"I [Watson] was standing at the Criterion Bar, when someone tapped me on the shoulder, and turning round I recognised young Stamford, who had been a dresser under me at Barts... I asked him to lunch with me at the Holborn, and we started off together in a Hansom." (ASIS)

It was shortly after this meeting, here, on New Years Day 1881, in what was then called the Criterion Bar, that Watson and Holmes were first introduced. Inside the Restaurant on the opposite wall to the bar is a "Watson and Holmes" commemorative wall plaque.

The Criterion is owned by celebrated chef, Marco Pierre White. It has been awarded 3 Michelin Stars and is an ideal stop for refreshments or a fine lunch.

Directions: Exit the Criterion Restaurant and walk to the other side of the Eros steps - to the traffic lights leading over Piccadilly Circus to the beginning of Regent Street. Approximately 30 metres up Regent Street at N° 68, on the right hand side, is the Café Royal ㉓

Café Royal: The Café Royal was founded in 1865 and was synonymous with artistic London of the 1880s. The Café Royal was patronised by the great writers and artists of that age, including Arthur Conan Doyle, Oscar Wilde, Max Beerbohm, Aubrey Beardsley and Augustus John.

"There are no exact details to hand, but the events seemed to have occurred at about 12.00 in Regent Street, outside the Café Royal. The attack was made by two men armed with sticks. Mr Holmes was beaten about the head and body... [The thugs] escaped the bystanders by passing through the Café Royal and out into Glasshouse Street behind it." (TIC)

Holmes was hurt and was carried to the Charing Cross Hospital ㉞

Directions: Return to Piccadilly Circus and the Eros statue. Continue past the Criterion Theatre and Restaurant and turn first right into Haymarket. Continue down the Haymarket, keeping on the left hand side. Stop at the Theatre Royal Haymarket ㉔

Theatre Royal Haymarket:

> *"'On that particular evening, old Amberly, wishing to give his wife*
> *a treat, had taken two upper circle seats at the Haymarket Theatre.*
> *At the last moment she had complained of a headache and had*
> *refused to go. He had gone alone ...' Watson."* (TRC)

Here Josiah Amberley claimed to have attended an evening performance at the Theatre Royal on the night of the disappearance of his wife. This incident supplied Holmes and Watson with their most brilliant pieces of deduction and sleuthing, which led to the conclusion of foul play and murder. A theatre has stood on this site from as early as 1720. The present Theatre was built in 1820 by John Nash.

Directions: Cross the road at the traffic lights and turn left down the Haymarket and walk past Her Majesty's Theatre until you arrive at Pall Mall. Cross the road at the lights, turn left and enter Cockspur Street.
Continue on the right, keeping Trafalgar Square on your left. Cross The Mall (which leads to Buckingham Palace). When on the other side, turn left and cross Whitehall. Turn right into Whitehall and continue on the left turning first left into Craig's Court ㉕

Craig's Court:

> *"Somewhere in the vaults of Cox & Co, at Charing Cross, there is a travel*
> *worn and battered despatch box with my name John H Watson, MD,*
> *late Indian Army, painted upon the lid. It is crammed with papers, nearly*
> *all of which are records of cases to illustrate the curious problems which*
> *Mr Sherlock Holmes had at various times to examine."* (TPOTB)

As you enter the Court, the building on your right was once the banking firm called Cox & Co. who were army agents and bankers.

As you exit the Court, notice the doorway on your right just before the narrow road leading out of the Court. This was the rear entrance to the Charing Cross Post Office:

> *"'You traced him through the telegram, no doubt', said Holmes. 'Exactly,*
> *Mr Holmes. We picked up the scent at the Charing Cross Post Office.'"*

Directions: Exit Craig's Court and turn left into Whitehall. Turn first left into Great Scotland Yard. The building immediately on your right was the former site of Scotland Yard ㉖

Former Site of Scotland Yard: Scotland Yard was the headquarters of the police force of metropolitan London. The street name (Great Scotland Yard) refers to a former palace for the Kings of Scotland, which was here 1000 years ago.

Directions: *Continue to the end of Great Scotland Yard. Cross Northumberland Avenue and turn left when on the other side of the road. A few metres further on the right is the Sherlock Holmes Pub* ㉗, *which is at the side of Craven Passage.*

Sherlock Holmes Pub:
In 1883, this building was called the Northumberland Hotel. It was in the Hotel that Sir Henry Baskerville lost one of his boots, while staying here as a guest in "The Hound of the Baskervilles" (THOTB). Later, the Hotel was renamed the Northumberland Arms.

"He laid an envelope on the table, and we all bent over it. It was of common quality, greyish colour. The address, 'Sir Henry Baskerville, Northumberland Hotel', was printed in rough characters; the post-mark 'Charing Cross' and the date of posting the preceding evening... 'Hum! Someone seems to be deeply interested in your movements'." (THOTB)

The Sherlock Holmes is a friendly pub, and an essential place to visit for anyone interested in Holmes and Watson. Why not try a glass of "Sherlock Holmes Ale" or have a meal in the restaurant, which overlooks the re-created famous Baker Street study?

The Pub walls are decorated with Sherlockian memorabilia and new items are constantly being added. There are many artefacts belonging to Holmes, including his large bowl pipe, violin, deerstalker, etc. The bust of Holmes, the one that reportedly decoyed an assassin's bullet, is next to the window. And to complete the fantasy, there is sample of soil from the Reichenback Falls, where Holmes encountered the evil Moriarty that fateful day.

Directions: *Exit the Pub. Turn left and enter the passage, which is called Craven Passage and stop at the first door on the right, which was the entrance to Neville's Turkish Baths* ㉘

Neville's Turkish Bath: This was the ladies' entrance to the Baths. The gentlemen's entrance, used by Holmes and Watson has long been demolished.

"Both Holmes and I had a weakness for the Turkish Bath. It was over a smoke in the pleasant lassitude of the drying-room that I found him less reticent and more human than anywhere else. On the upper floor of the Northumberland Avenue establishment there is a solid corner where two couches lie side by side." (TIC)

Directions: *Continue to the end of Craven Passage and stop at the junction with Craven Street.*

Craven Street: *"They lodged, I find, at the Mexborough Private Hotel, in Craven Street, which was actually one of those called upon by my agent in search of evidence. Here he kept his wife imprisoned in her room while he, disguised in a beard, followed Dr Mortimer to Baker Street."* (THOTB)

This Street has changed little since the 19th century and the model for the Mexborough Hotel was probably a real hotel called the Craven Family Hotel. The exact number of the Mexborough Hotel, like many other places in the stories, was never identified, although a Craven Hotel has been identified at N°s 43-46. At N° 36 Craven Street, Benjamin Franklin had his London home.

Directions: Turn left into Craven Street and continue on the right until you reach the Strand. Stop here and look to your right up the Strand 🔵29

The Strand: It was along this section of the Strand that Holmes, Watson and Watson's pooch would perambulate for hours at a time,

> *"watching the ever changing Kaleidoscope of life,*
> *ebbing and flowing around them."* (TFP)

It was also between here and Charing Cross Station (further along on your right) where Dr Watson was: *"stunned for some moments"* by *"the terrible news-sheet"* displayed by *"a one-legged news vendor"* which said: *"MURDEROUS ATTACK UPON SHERLOCK HOLMES."* (TIC)

Directions: Turn right; walk a little further to Charing Cross Train Station 🔵30

Charing Cross Train Station: *"'Come, Watson, Come!' he cried. 'The game is afoot. Not a word! Into your clothes and come!' Ten minutes later we were both in a cab and rattling through the silent streets on our way to Charing Cross Station."* (TAG)

The Station was built in 1864 and has played a prominent role in the Canon. It was from Charing Cross Station that Holmes and Watson departed to investigate the mysteries of the Abbey Grange. Here also, in the Station waiting room, Holmes had an altercation with a man named Mathews who knocked out Holmes' left canine tooth (TEH).

Directions: Outside Charing Cross Train Station, on the left, where the traffic lights are at present, stood the American Exchange Stand 🔵31

American Exchange Stand: In "A Study in Scarlet" (ASIS), two letters were found on the body of Enoch Drebber. The letters were marked: **"To be left until called for"**, and were addressed to the **"American Exchange Strand"**.

Directions: By Charing Cross Train Station is the Charing Cross Hotel 🔵32

Charing Cross Hotel: It was in the Hotel's smoking room that Holmes set a trap for murderer and spy Hugo Oberstein, and thus secured the safe return of the missing papers belonging to Bruce Partington in "The Bruce Partington Plans":

> *"I shall expect to meet you in the smoking room of the*
> *Charing Cross Hotel at noon on Saturday. Remember that only*
> *English notes, or gold, will be taken."* (TBPP)

Directions: Opposite Charing Cross Train Station at N° 440 Strand, the large glass building is the Coutt's and Co Bank **33**

Coutt's and Co Bank: The Bank was founded in 1692 and is the largest private bank in the country - most famous because Royalty, including our present Queen and members of the Royal household, are customers. The present Coutt's and Co building occupies the former site of the Lowther Arcade.

> *"Into his Hansom you will jump, and will drive to the Strand*
> *end of the Lowther Arcade... and the instant your cab stops,*
> *dash through the Arcade, timing yourself."* (TFP)

The Lowther Arcade was originally built in 1831. It was here that Watson was made to run, from the Strand entrance, through the Arcade, to be picked up in Adelaide Street by Mycroft Holmes, who was waiting in a Brougham cab. It was also here that Holmes bought his Stradivarius violin in "The Final Problem" (TFP).

Directions: Cross the Strand at the traffic lights in front of you. Turn right when on the other side of the road and turn into the first road on the left which is Agar Street. Notice the yellow triangular building in the angle between William IV Street and Agar Street. This was once the Charing Cross Hospital **34**. *Today it is Charing Cross Police Station.*

Charing Cross Hospital: Sherlock Holmes was brought here after being beaten up by Baron Adelbert Gruner's hired ruffians outside the Café Royal **23**, in "The Illustrious Client" (TIC). The Hospital was founded in 1818.

> *"The attack was made by two men armed with sticks, and Mr Holmes, was*
> *beaten about the head and body, receiving injuries which the doctors*
> *describe as most serious. He was carried to Charing Cross Hospital."* (TIC)

Directions: Return to the Strand and turn left. Stop at N° 418 Strand, which is today a retail shop, but was George Hy Harris's Shop **35**

George Hy Harris's Shop: This building has been identified as the shop where Sir Henry Baskerville bought his half lost tan boots in "The Hound of the Baskervilles" (THOTB).

Directions: Continue and stop at the Adelphi Theatre **36***, at N° 413 Strand.*

Adelphi Theatre: According to Conan Doyle's autobiography "Memories and Adventures ", it was at the Adelphi Theatre, in 1924, that Conan Doyle staged his dramatisation of "Rodney Stone" and re-named it "The House of Temperley". No one would finance the venture as it was seen as too great a financial risk, so Conan Doyle sub-let the Theatre himself for six months. The new production was a disaster so, in desperation and in record time, he wrote and rehearsed "The Speckled Band" and saved the day.

Directions: Continue along the Strand on the left until the corner of Exeter Street. Opposite you, on the other side of the Strand, is the Savoy Hotel **37**

Savoy Hotel: This world-famous Hotel stands on the site of the Savoy Palace; the Palace was built in 1214. The first manager of the Savoy Hotel was Cesar Ritz, who later founded the famous Ritz Hotel. Cesar Ritz later tragically lost all his fortune at the Ritz Hotel, when asked to organise Edward VII's Coronation banquet. The Coronation was cancelled 48 hours before the start, due to the King developing appendicitis. Ritz lost a fortune and suffered a nervous breakdown, from which he never recovered.

Famous guests include Monet (who used to sit and paint "Thames fogs" from the fifth floor) and, aspiring US President, Hoover (who set up a rent-free office in the Hotel to repatriate 120,000 Americans stranded in Europe at the outbreak of the First World War).

Directions: Just a little further along to the left of the Savoy Hotel, at N° 100 Strand, is the famous restaurant "Simpson's in the Strand" **38**

Simpson's In the Strand:
"I met Holmes at Simpson's that evening and we looked down on the rushing stream of life in the Strand from a small table near the front window." (TIC).
This was one of Holmes and Watson's favourite restaurants; they dined here twice in "The Illustrious Client" (TIC) and "took something nutritious" here after the arrest of Culverton Smith in "The Dying Detective".

Simpson's has specialised in traditional English cooking (notably roast beef) since Victorian times.

Directions: Continue along the Strand and turn first left into Burleigh Street. Keep on the right side and cross Exeter Street. Immediately on your right is N° 12 Burleigh Street **39**

Nº 12 Burleigh Street: This Building is effectively the holy shrine to the true Sherlockian - the birthplace of many of the Sherlock Holmes stories. The "Strand Magazine" had its first issues published from this address and pictured "Burleigh Street" on the front cover of the Magazine.

Directions: Return to the Strand and turn left. Continue and turn left into Wellington Street and immediately on the left is the Lyceum Theatre **40**

Lyceum Theatre:
> *"'Be at the third pillar from the left outside the Lyceum Theatre tonight at seven o'clock... You are a wronged woman and shall have justice. Do not bring police... ' Your unknown friend. "* (TSOF).

It was at the Lyceum Theatre (constructed in 1771) that Mary Morstan, after receiving a mysterious note, was requested to meet one of the Sholoto gang, the secret benefactors, who had mysteriously posted her one large pearl each year, for the past six years. It was at the third pillar from the left that Holmes, Watson and Mary Morstan met, before sharing a four-wheeler and heading up Wellington Street in "The Sign Of Four (TSOF).

Directions: Continue on the left up Wellington Street. Keep to the left and cross Russell Street, where the road becomes Bow Street. Continue, and a little further on the left, is the New Royal Opera House **41**

Royal Opera House: The Opera House was completed in 1858. Holmes visited the Opera House frequently, especially when one of Richard Wagner's operas was performed:
> *"By the way, it is not eight o'clock, and a Wagner night at Covent Garden! If we hurry, we might be in time for the second act."* (TRC)

Directions: On the opposite side of the road, to the left, is the Bow Street Police Court **42**

Bow Street Police Court: In "The Man With A Twisted Lip" (TMWTL), Holmes hurried to the cells here, to wash Hugh Boone's face and so solve the mystery of the disappearance of Neville St Clair:
> *"'Well, I don't know why not', said the inspector. 'He doesn't look a credit to the Bow Street cells, does he?' He slipped his key into the lock... Holmes stooped to the water jug, moistened his sponge, and then rubbed it twice vigorously across and down the prisoner's face."*